Library Research with Emergent Readers:
Meeting Standards Through Collaboration

Christa Harker
and
Dorette Putonti

Linworth
Books

Professional Development Resources for K–12
Library Media and Technology Specialists

Library of Congress Cataloging-in-Publication Data

Harker, Christa.

 Library research with emergent readers : meeting standards through collaboration / Christa Harker and
Dorette Putonti.

    p. cm.

 Includes bibliographical references and index.

  ISBN-13: 978-1-58683-288-9 (pbk.)

  ISBN-10: 1-58683-288-3 (pbk.)

 1. Library orientation for school children. 2. Research--Study and teaching (Primary)--Activity programs.
3. Information literacy--Study and teaching (Primary)--Activity programs. 4. Elementary school libraries--
Activity programs. 5. School librarian participation in curriculum planning. 6. Education--Standards--United
States. I. Putonti, Dorette. II. Title.

  Z711.25.S36H37 2008

  027.62'5--dc22

                                    2007042179

Cynthia Anderson: Editor
Carol Simpson: Editorial Director
Judi Repman: Consulting Editor

Published by Linworth Publishing, Inc.
3650 Olentangy River Road
Suite 250
Columbus, Ohio 43214

ISBN 13: 978-1-58683-288-9
ISBN 10: 1-58683-288-3

5 4 3 2 1

Table of Contents

Table of Figures

About the Authors

Christa Harker has been the librarian at James Bowie Elementary School, a kindergarten through sixth grade school in Dallas, since 1996. Christa holds an MLIS and a BA in English from the University of Texas at Austin. Her frequent library and educator conference presentations highlight the integration of information literacy skills with classroom curriculum, teacher and librarian collaboration, and student reading motivation.

Dorette Putonti has been the librarian at Hamilton Park Pacesetter Magnet School in Dallas, Texas, since 1995. She earned her MLS at Texas Woman's University and her BA in English at Bloomfield College. Dorette often presents at library and educator conferences on professional learning communities, mentoring, and teacher and librarian collaboration.

Acknowledgments

The ideas and projects in this book have been nine years in the making. We are deeply indebted to the teachers at our schools for their collaboration and professionalism. These teachers include Cindy Whitten, Christie Isom, Mary Tanner, Ashley Stephenson, and many others. Our past and present directors of libraries have supported us throughout the years with flexibility, resources, and presentation opportunities; thank you Thelma Gay, Karen Shull, and Julie Briggs. We would also like to acknowledge the professional support of the other librarians in the Richardson Independent School District. Finally, we would like to thank our families for their patience and love.

Introduction

This manual is designed to provide practical guidance to librarians and teachers ready to collaborate in order to tackle library research with emergent readers, students in kindergarten, first grade, and second grade who are in the beginning stages of learning to read. The manual integrates national curriculum standards with information literacy standards to address the instructional needs of the classroom teacher and the librarian, and student assessments. Best instructional practices are incorporated into the lessons for teacher and librarian use, allowing for differentiated instruction to meet various learning styles and needs. Each research project included incorporates research-based instructional strategies and curriculum content taught around the nation.

We have spent the last nine years developing the ideas and projects included in this manual. Each project has been taught in one or both of our school libraries. Each year we continue to adapt, enhance, and rework our ideas to include better instructional timing, higher-level thinking skills, more appropriate resources, and opportunities for individual modifications and extensions. In short, these projects are still works in progress. They will always be works in progress as educational research continues to examine how students learn best.

MANUAL ORGANIZATION

Chapter 1 provides the educational research and justification for library research with emergent readers. Many teachers, content curriculum specialists, and librarians believe that library research with students who are just beginning to develop their reading skills is a futile endeavor. These students, however, are often the most enthusiastic, curious, and diligent researchers to visit the school library. After nine years of conducting library research with emergent readers, we often wonder, "Why aren't more people doing this in their school libraries?" Chapter 1 provides the educational foundation to encourage other librarians and teachers to try library research with emergent readers.

Chapter 2 gives the step-by-step process for conducting library research with emergent readers. Important instructional strategies and procedural information are included in this chapter. Specific instructions for differentiated instruction and ideas to incorporate higher-level thinking skills are highlighted.

The remainder of this manual contains research projects that can be used with emergent readers in a variety of situations. Each project is aligned with national content curriculum standards and information literacy standards. These projects have been used with emergent readers in kindergarten, first grade, and second grade. Users of this manual may copy and use the research examples provided or modify them to fit their instructional needs. A library research project collaboration checklist, sample assessment rubrics, and a matrix highlighting connections to a variety of national curriculum standards are also included.

A Works Cited list will provide readers with additional resources for developing their own library research projects for emergent readers.

TABLE 1.2 MATRIX OF CONTENT STANDARDS INTEGRATION

Content Standards	Animals Chapter 3	Earth Features Chapter 4	Seasons Chapter 5	Plants Chapter 6	Community Helpers Chapter 7	American Symbols Chapter 8	Five Senses Chapter 9
Benchmarks for Language Arts by Mid-continent Research for Education and Learning www.mcrel.org/standards-benchmarks							
Standard 1: Writing Process	•	•	•	•	•	•	•
Standard 4: Research Process	•	•	•	•	•	•	•
Standard 5: Reading Process	•	•	•	•	•	•	•
Standard 6: Variety of Texts	•	•	•	•	•	•	•
Standard 7: Informational Text	•	•	•	•	•	•	•
Standard 9: Visual Media	•	•	•	•	•	•	•
Standards for the English Language Arts by National Council of Teachers of English and International Reading Association www.ncte.org							
Standard 1: Reading to Build Understanding	•	•	•	•	•	•	•
Standard 3: Reading Strategies	•	•	•	•	•	•	•
Standard 5: Writing Process	•	•	•	•	•	•	•
Standard 7: Research Process	•	•	•	•	•	•	•
Standard 8: Variety of Resources	•	•	•	•	•	•	•
Information Literacy Standards for Student Learning by American Association of School Librarians and Association for Educational Communications and Technology http://www.ala.org/ala/aasl/aaslproftools/informationpower/InformationLiteracyStandards_final.pdf							
Standard 1: Information Access	•	•	•	•	•	•	•
Standard 2: Information Evaluation	•	•	•	•	•	•	•
Standard 3: Use of Information	•	•	•	•	•	•	•
National Science Education Standards: K-4 by National Committee on Science Education Standards and Assessment, National Research Council www.nap.edu/readingroom/books/nses/6c.html							
Standard A: Science as Inquiry	•	•	•	•			•
Standard C: Life Science	•			•			•
Standard D: Earth and Space Science		•	•				
Curriculum Standards for Social Studies by National Council for the Social Studies http://www.socialstudies.org/standards/							
III: People, Places, & Environments		•	•				
VI: Power, Authority, & Governance						•	
VII: Production, Distribution, & Consumption					•		
National Educational Technology Standards for Students by International Society for Technology in Education http://cnets.iste.org/							
2. Copyright Issues	•	•	•	•	•	•	•
3. Productivity		•				•	•
4. Communications		•				•	•
5. Research							•
6. Problem-Solving		•				•	•

LIBRARY RESEARCH PROJECT PLANNING AND COLLABORATION CHECKLIST

Figure B.1 Planning Worksheet

Planning Worksheet
Research for Emergent Readers

Research Project Title:

Grade Level: Date for project:

Length of time in classroom:
Length of time in library:
Length of time in computer lab:

Instructional Goals
What do you want the students to learn during this research project?

How will you assess student success?

How will you integrate technology into this research project?

Will students work individually, in pairs, in small groups, or as a class?

Instructional Standards
Which content standards are the main focus for this research project?

Which information literacy standards are the main focus for this project?

Which other content standards will be integrated into this project?

❑ Early Literacy   ❑ Math
❑ Language Arts   ❑ Technology
❑ Science   ❑ Art
❑ Social Studies   ❑ Music
❑ _____   ❑ _____

Collaboration Checklist
Complete attached collaboration checklist prior to the research project.

- -

Project Evaluation
Reflect on these questions after the research project is completed.
Were instructional goals met? Why or why not?

What worked well during this project?

What needs to be changed for the next project?

From *Library Research with Emergent Readers: Meeting Standards through Collaboration* by Christa Harker and Dorette Putonti. Columbus, OH: Linworth Publishing, Inc. Copyright © 2008.

Collaboration Checklist
Research for Emergent Readers

Research Project Title:

Grade Level: Date for project:

Task	Librarian	Teacher
Create student note-taking organizer (booklet, worksheet, graphic organizer)		
Create assessment rubric		
Gather research sources (books, web sites, online resources, encyclopedias, etc.)		
Gather materials (crayons, pencils, sticky notes, etc.)		
Copy student note-taking organizer		
Teach introductory content needed		
Teach research/information literacy skills needed		
Teach technology skills needed		
Monitor student progress		
Assess student success		
Evaluate project for future use		

From *Library Research with Emergent Readers: Meeting Standards through Collaboration* by Christa Harker and Dorette Putonti. Columbus, OH: Linworth Publishing, Inc. Copyright © 2008.

chapter 1

Background Research

WHY DO LIBRARY RESEARCH WITH EMERGENT READERS?

- **Integrate and teach information literacy skills**
- **Provide opportunities for meaningful librarian-teacher collaboration**
- **Incorporate higher-level thinking skills**
- **Differentiate instruction**
- **Integrate content curriculum standards**

Many teachers and librarians are skeptical when it comes to conducting library research with children who are just learning to read. Fortunately, these students have natural curiosity that makes research and the discovery of new information an exciting adventure, even if their reading skills are not fully developed. This library research is also an opportunity for children to apply a variety of skills that have been taught in isolation within the classroom. Library research offers a prime opportunity to integrate a wide variety of content curriculum, early literacy skills, information literacy skills, and higher-level thinking skills.

In *Powering Achievement: School Library Media Programs Make a Difference*, Keith Curry Lance and David Loertscher discuss the impact high quality libraries have on student academic success. According to the authors, high quality librarians participate in three important activities:

- **collaborating with teachers to create learning experiences;**
- **teaching information literacy; and**
- **promoting reading.**

Two of these activities are directly addressed through library research: collaboration between teachers and librarians to create quality learning integrating a variety of materials and technology, and teaching information literacy skills. The third activity, promoting reading, is an extension of library research—students are exposed to nonfiction material, which many find interesting and desirable for pleasure reading.

INFORMATION LITERACY INTEGRATION

Library research with emergent readers begins the challenging task of teaching information literacy at a young age. Instructional attention is focused on building a foundation of life-long learning for the youngest students. Emergent reader library research encompasses key components of the American

Association of School Librarians' *Standards for the 21st-Century Learner*, where "learners use skills, resources, and tools to:

1. Inquire, think critically, and gain knowledge.
2. Draw conclusions, make informed decisions, apply knowledge to new situations, and create new knowledge.
3. Share knowledge and participate ethically and productively as members of our democratic society.
4. Pursue personal and aesthetic growth."

Used with permission of American Library Association

Additionally, the following standards and indicators from *Information Literacy Standards for Student Learning* are actively taught during library research with emergent readers. The instructional goal through research is to have the students meet the basic level of proficiency for each standard, as determined by age appropriateness.

Standard 1. The student who is information literate accesses information efficiently and effectively.

- Indicator 1. Recognizes the need for information
- Indicator 2. Recognizes that accurate and comprehensive information is the basis for intelligent decision making
- Indicator 3. Formulates questions based on information needs
- Indicator 4. Identifies a variety of potential sources of information
- Indicator 5. Develops and uses successful strategies for locating information

Standard 2. The student who is information literate evaluates information critically and competently.

- Indicator 4. Selects information appropriate to the problem or question at hand

Standard 3. The student who is information literate uses information accurately and creatively.

- Indicator 1. Organizes information for practical application
- Indicator 2. Integrates new information into one's own knowledge
- Indicator 3. Applies information in critical thinking and problem solving
- Indicator 4. Produces and communicates information and ideas in appropriate formats

Used with permission of American Library Association

TEACHER/LIBRARIAN COLLABORATION

In *Powering Achievement*, the authors explained that the Colorado studies of 2000 and many state assessment studies thereafter noted a correlation between quality librarian and teacher collaboration and student academic achievement.

Library research gives librarians and teachers an opportunity to collaborate to meet a wide variety of instructional goals. Teachers are able to address important content curriculum and early literacy skills, while librarians are able to introduce important information literacy skills such as recognizing an information need; using a problem-solving process; accessing, analyzing, and interpreting information based on a need; and effectively communicating information.

HIGHER-LEVEL THINKING SKILLS

David V. Loertscher, et al., stresses in *Ban Those Bird Units: 15 Models for Teaching and Learning in Information-rich and Technology-rich Environments* that library research must incorporate skills that go beyond cutting and pasting information. Students must be challenged to use higher-level thinking to expand and deepen their learning experiences. A carefully designed library research project easily incorporates quality instructional strategies that engage and challenge students to analyze, synthesize, and evaluate information. This manual provides these higher-level thinking skills integrated within library research.

DIFFERENTIATED INSTRUCTION

Library research also allows for differentiated instructional strategies. Students can conduct their research individually; in homogeneous group/pairs; in heterogeneous group/pairs; or in a whole group, small group, or pair led by an adult or older-mentor student. Many of the research units designed in this manual rely on instructional strategies that are appropriate for English language learners and special education students as well as gifted and talented learners.

Robert J. Marzano points out in *What Works in Schools: Translating Research into Action* that there are nine categories of instructional strategies that are most affective in stretching student achievement (82-83). (Refer to Figure 1.1, Instructional Strategies That Affect Student Achievement by Robert J. Marzano, at the end of this chapter for more information.) Library research is an opportunity to use effective instructional strategies such as comparing, contrasting, classifying, note-taking, summarizing, graphing, and organizing information gained through research. Students must work through Bloom's Taxonomy (Figure 1.2, Taxonomy for Learning, Teaching, and Assessing) and a problem-solving process (Figure 1.3, Problem-Solving Processes), such as "The Big6™" or "The Super3™," which allow students with different needs to conduct research at their individual instructional level. Each of the research units in this manual will give examples illustrating how to make modifications for individual learning styles.

CURRICULUM STANDARDS INTEGRATION

CONTENT CURRICULUM STANDARDS

Teachers want to know what library research can do for them. They have limited time with their students, and the pressure they are under for student achievement is enormous! It is important to highlight for teachers how library research with their youngest students is beneficial in addressing specific content curriculum.

- **Library research provides natural connections to science and social studies content.**
- **Research can be used as an introductory point for a unit, developing background knowledge on an upcoming topic or lesson.**

- **Research can be used as an extension of content when the students are engaged in the lesson topic and want to learn more.**
- **Research enables students to make connections to the world around them.**

LANGUAGE ARTS/EARLY LITERACY SKILLS STANDARDS

Research is also an important opportunity for students to apply their early literacy skills that they have learned in the classroom in a real world situation. They have an information need and they will need to use their literacy skills to locate and analyze the information in order to meet their need. During library research, students will access information textually and graphically in a resource, decide which information meets their need, write their notes on a graphic organizer, summarize what they have learned through their research, and then synthesize and apply the new knowledge.

Library research with emergent readers integrates the Language Arts benchmarks listed by Mid-continent Research for Education and Learning for Level Pre-K (Grades Pre-K) and Level I (Grades K-2), as well as the Standards for the English Language Arts sponsored by NCTE and IRA. (Language Arts/Early Literacy standards and benchmarks connected to library research with emergent readers are listed in Table 1.2, Matrix of Content Standards Integration. For specific standards and benchmarks, please visit each organization's Web site, which are listed in Works Cited.)

TECHNOLOGY

Library research also provides a logical and effective way to apply technology skills. Research allows practical opportunities for students to use technology in the research process by introducing information acquisition through online resources, Web sites (many of which contain audio and graphical information), streaming videos, and other technologies. Many of the content videos available through Discovery Education *streaming* <http://streaming.discoveryeducation.com/> (formerly *United Streaming*), a subscription video streaming service, will support and enhance the research projects included in this manual. An online encyclopedia, such as *World Book Kids* <http://worldbookonline.com/>, will provide experience with subject searching in order to locate a picture or appropriate graphic to go along with printed source information. (Note, both Discovery Education *streaming* and *World Book Kids* require subscriptions.) Finally, online games can creatively support what the students have learned during their research and provide them with the opportunity to apply their new knowledge.

Library research also provides an avenue for students to create their final product using such computer programs as Kid Pix® or Kidspiration®. Students can use their developing technology skills to draw pictures, create webs, add text, and insert from pre-selected images to create a variety of products. This technology integration may include collaboration with a technology specialist, if one is available on your campus.

Figure 1.1 Instructional Strategies That Affect Student Achievement by Robert J. Marzano

Instructional Strategies That Affect Student Achievement
By Robert J. Marzano

Robert J. Marzano's *What Works in Schools: Translating Research into Action* highlights nine affective instructional strategies. When planning research for emergent readers, keep in mind the most effective instructional strategies.

1. Identifying Similarities and Differences
   - Comparing
   - Classifying
   - Creating metaphors and analogies

2. Summarizing and Note Taking
   - Verbal notes
   - Written notes (textual and pictorial)

3. Reinforcing Effort and Providing Recognition
   - Reinforce during project
   - Recognize effort after project

4. Homework and Practice
   - Consistent practice of research skills and strategies

5. Nonlinguistic Representations
   - Creating pictures, graphic organizers, models, charts, graphs, and demonstrations

6. Cooperative Learning
   - Cooperative peer pairs/groups
   - Ability pairs/groups
   - Mentor student pairs/groups

7. Setting Objectives and Providing Feedback
   - Summative assessment
   - Formative assessment
   - Self assessment

8. Generating and Testing Hypothesis

9. Questions, Cues, and Advance Organizers
   - Review what is already known
   - Link to previous knowledge
   - Provide organizers for new content

Figure 1.2 Taxonomy for Learning, Teaching, and Assessing

Taxonomy for Learning, Teaching, and Assessing

Bloom's Taxonomy provides a framework for creating educational objectives. Included in this appendix are the original framework and the revised framework. When creating educational objectives for research with emergent readers, it is important to consider objectives that require higher-level thinking skills and problem solving strategies appropriate for the age group.

Original Bloom's Taxonomy Framework

Knowledge
Comprehension
Application
Analysis
Synthesis
Evaluation

Revised Framework of Bloom's Taxonomy
(Cognitive Process Dimension)

Remember
Understand
Apply
Analyze
Evaluate
Create

Taxonomy for Learning, Teaching, and Assessing Cognitive Process Dimension

Table 1.3 Cognitive Process Dimension

Remember	recognizing and recalling
Understand	interpreting, exemplifying, classifying, summarizing, inferring, comparing, and explaining
Apply	executing and implementing
Analyze	differentiating, organizing, and attributing
Evaluate	checking and critiquing
Create	generating, planning, and producing

From Anderson, Lorin W., David R. Krathohl, et al. *Taxonomy for Learning, Teaching and Assessing, A: A Revision of Bloom's Taxonomy of Educational Objectives, Complete Edition*,1/e. Published by Allyn and Bacon, Boston, MA. Copyright © 2001 by Pearson Eduction. Reprinted by permission of the publisher.

Figure 1.3 Problem-Solving Processes

Problem-Solving Processes

The Big6™ and the Super3™ are two examples of problem-solving processes that work well with emergent readers during library research. It is important to choose a problem-solving process and to use it consistently with the students as they progress in their research skills yearly.

The Super3™

1. Plan my job.
2. Do my job.
3. Review my work.

The Big6™

1. What job do I need to do? What do I need to know?
2. Which resources can I use to do my job?
3. Where do I find the resources I need?
4. What information can I use? How do I record this information?
5. What should I create with the information I have learned?
6. How can I make sure I have done my best work?

The Big6™ and the Super3™ are copyrighted by Michael Eisenberg and Robert Berkowitz.

Eisenberg, Michael B. and Robert E. Berkowitz. *Teaching Information & Technology Skills: The Big6 in Elementary Schools*. Worthington, OH: Linworth Publishing, Inc. 1999.

chapter 2

The Step-by-Step Process of Research with Emergent Readers

STEP-BY-STEP EMERGENT READER RESEARCH

Listed below are steps to consider when approaching a teacher for first-time library research with emergent readers. A sample planning worksheet and collaboration checklist in Appendix B of this manual incorporates these steps.

1. **Brainstorm possible research topics focusing on classroom curriculum and standards. Work to logically integrate content curriculum, information literacy skills, and technology.**

2. **Consider the instructional timing of your research. Review available print and electronic resources for age and subject appropriateness.**

3. **Approach the teacher with your research idea, sample projects, and resources.**

4. **Develop a project plan that incorporates research skills targeted, including a problem-solving process. Consider differentiated instruction in content, process, and product.**

5. **Decide on a student product. Ensure that students are required to think beyond basic information gathering.**

6. **Gather the student materials needed for the research project.**

7. **Teach students any necessary information literacy skills prior to research time, such as a problem-solving process or use of a bibliography. Work with students during research time and as they complete their product.**

8. **Complete rubrics to determine student success and to ensure instructional goals have been met.**

9. **Evaluate and modify the project for future use.**

STEP 1 - BRAINSTORMING

Brainstorm possible research topics focusing on classroom curriculum and standards.
Work to logically integrate content curriculum, information literacy skills, and technology.

Depending on your relationship with the teacher and the teacher's enthusiasm for this project, you may decide to work with the teacher from step one, or wait until a later step to approach the teacher with your library research project ideas. During the brainstorming process, keep in mind the teacher's instructional goals and the library's information literacy goals. Be sure to use required curriculum standards as the foundation for the library research project.

Forcing content and skills integration will make for a confusing and frustrating library research project. Make sure that the curriculum, information literacy skills, and technology skills flow in a logical sequence. Take into account the content and skills already taught in the classroom, library, and technology lab. You may not be able to teach every skill through one library research project. Focus on the content and skills that work together.

STEP 2 - INSTRUCTIONAL TIMING

Consider the instructional timing of your research. Review available print and electronic resources for age and subject appropriateness.

These are several questions to ask yourself in relation to instructional timing.

- **Is it the beginning of the school year?**
- **Do the students know how to write their letters, or would it be better for the students to take notes by drawing pictures of their information?**
- **Do the students have a routine for coming to work in the library?**

Answers to these questions will affect the length of the project, the resources the students use, the format for note-taking, and whether students work individually or in groups.

Choosing appropriate resources for library research is a critical component of a successful research project with emergent readers. The librarian should review all student resources to ensure that important information is addressed pictorially as well as textually and will not cause the emergent or non-reader frustration or anxiety. Because emergent readers are still developing their reading skills, these young researchers often need to interpret a source's pictures in order to answer their research needs. Appropriate sources should include text that is simply written and factual. Additionally, sources containing a table of contents and index are helpful when introducing research skills to emergent readers.

Gather a representative selection of sources for the teacher to review. Teachers may be unaware of the wide variety of nonfiction resources available for emergent readers. Providing a selection to reference during the collaboration will help the teacher visualize how library research with emergent readers may be conducted.

Several publishers have recently added nonfiction series aimed at emergent and beginning readers. Student Resources for Primary Research Projects, Appendix C, lists several of these series that may be used as sources for new library research projects. Sources with more difficult text but quality pictures are also helpful. Check for consistency in content covered and organization of text when choosing a series where each student will research a different topic and use a different book from the series. (See Appendix C, Table C.1, Student Resources for Primary Research Projects, for example publishers and series.)

STEP 3 - TEACHER COLLABORATION

Approach the teacher with your research idea, sample projects, and resources.

The first challenge to library research with emergent readers is convincing a teacher to collaborate with the librarian. Using David Loertscher's *Taxonomies of the School Library Media Program*, the collaboration level necessary between a teacher and librarian to plan, develop, execute, and evaluate a library research project for emergent readers could reach Levels 8-10 of the *School Library Media Specialist Taxonomy*, depending on the partnership between the teacher and librarian.

For this desired high-level of collaboration, it is best to be fully armed with in-depth knowledge of the required curriculum and standards before approaching a teacher. Incorporating a teacher's ideas and feedback will help include the teacher in planning a research project. The teacher is the expert on her student's abilities, and her advice on the modifications and extensions should be incorporated into the project. Additionally, keep in mind the librarian's and teacher's roles during a collaboration.

LIBRARIAN ROLE

Process is the primary responsibility of the librarian. The librarian should teach lessons on how to locate and record information, and how to research for an information need (a problem-solving process). The librarian should also evaluate the resources needed and monitor student progress during the research project. Often during collaboration, the librarian is responsible for helping the teacher integrate content and for creating materials for student use during research, such as graphic organizers to aid students in taking notes.

TEACHER ROLE

Content, with an eye to curriculum standards, is the primary responsibility of the teacher. The teacher of record is responsible for teaching content, and monitoring and assessing student progress based on differentiated instructional needs. The teacher may also be responsible for parental communication, if needed.

It is important to incorporate the teacher's ideas and suggestions into the library research project. Discuss with the teacher any skills or knowledge that need to be introduced to the students prior to their library research time. Decide who is responsible for teaching these skills and when they should be taught. Bring the library schedule to the teacher to facilitate lesson and research scheduling.

STEP 4 - PROJECT PLANNING

Develop a project plan that incorporates research skills targeted, including a problem-solving process. Consider differentiated instruction in content, process, and product.

Because students are developing their background knowledge of how to conduct library research, it is important to introduce a problem-solving process during their first library research lessons. Skills introduced at this age are ones the students will internalize more quickly when they are older. It is important for students to realize that they are:

- **Going through a process that involves identifying an information need;**
- **Determining the sources they will use to help them answer their need;**
- **Deciding how they are going to record the information; and,**
- **Creating a bibliography for the information they deem appropriate to their need.**

Additionally, students will synthesize their information to answer the information need and evaluate their success at answering their information need. There are many problem-solving models in use by librarians, all of which may be modified to use with the emergent reader.

Research with emergent readers is a prime opportunity to develop other introductory research skills. Students will be building their background knowledge of what research is and how research is done. For example, during the problem-solving process, have students brainstorm the kinds of information they would like to discover through their research. Young children often need to learn how to develop appropriate research questions. Modeling how to develop strong research questions—questions that require more than a yes-or-no answer—takes time, but will become an invaluable part of the students' later research process. For example, leading students to ask "How does this animal move?" or "How many legs does this animal have?" instead of "Does this animal have legs?" will lead them toward in-depth questioning and research when they are older.

The research skills addressed during a library research project will determine the format for student note-taking, bibliography, instructional grouping, and individual modifications and extensions. Questions to consider include:

- How will students take notes?
- How will they record their bibliography?
- Will they work in groups, pairs, or individually?
- Will the librarian or teacher lead a whole group research investigation?
- Are there individual modifications or extensions to be made?

RESEARCH FORMAT
Decide how students will record their research notes. Keep in mind the instructional timing of the library project. Whether the students are drawing, circling, or writing their information determines the type of note-taking organizer you will provide for the students. Instructional timing will also determine whether the students will work individually or in groups, and whether each student is responsible for taking his own notes or taking notes as a group. Also keep in mind the group dynamics when deciding how long the students will spend conducting their library research. Will the class be able to work in one or two longer sessions (45 minutes to an hour)? Or, would it be better to break up the research time into short 20-30 minute blocks of time?

RESEARCH SKILLS
When young students come to the library for their first research experience, it is important to discuss with them what research is and what it isn't. Students will be tempted to answer their research notes with information they already know (or think they know).

TIP: Having students take out their "magic mind erasers" to temporarily erase the information they already know about a topic is a fun way to work on this skill.

PROVE IT
Additionally, asking students to "prove it" is a useful step to ensure that students are using their sources to find the information they need. When proving the information in their notes, they simply turn to the picture or page where they found the information and explain to the librarian how they found their answer. This procedure also allows the librarian to follow the thought process of the student as he conducts research. Proving it is a formative assessment that occurs during library research and note-taking time.

Finally, pointing out that researchers need to give credit to their sources is critical to introducing bibliographies or work cited lists. One way to incorporate this skill is to explain to the students that they need to prove that their answers were found in a source. People reading or viewing their research project will need to know that they conducted research. Because they cannot always have the actual source when showing their project to someone else, they can write down the title and author of the source that they used instead. A bibliography proves to others that research was done.

MODIFICATIONS TO INCLUDE ALL CHILDREN (DIFFERENTIATED INSTRUCTION)

The research projects in this manual may be adapted to meet specific learning needs. For students in special education or English Language Learners, more drawing and less writing may be an appropriate instructional modification. For gifted and talented students, adding a variety of resources and requiring complete sentences may add the needed challenges. Below are some possible modifications and extensions for library research with emergent readers.

Modifications

★ Require less writing—have students draw their research notes

★ Vary resources according to instructional level

★ Use highlight tape or sticky notes to highlight information in text to aid student in writing answers

★ Ensure all information needed can be found using only the source's pictures

★ Read pages to individuals, as needed

★ Pace whole class through note-taking, reading each page aloud

★ Transcribe student's verbal answers

★ Partner students with a research mentor from an older grade level

★ Group students in high/low pairs or small groups

★ Read resource to student (or class) while student(s) take notes

★ Take notes as a class, with students providing information to record in the class research notes

Extensions

★ Ensure some information needed must be answered using a source's text, requiring some reading

★ Require more writing. Have students write using a complete sentence or more fill-in-the-blank answers

★ Introduce the Table of Contents and Index to students for use during their research

★ Ask students to create their own note-taking booklet, which includes additional research

★ Add additional resources according to instructional level, such as an online encyclopedia or Web site. Have student conduct a subject search, locate appropriate pictures, and print them out

★ Have students research more than one of the topics and then compare the research information that is discovered

---

STEP 5 - STUDENT RESEARCH PROJECTS

Decide on a student product. Ensure that students are required to think beyond basic information gathering.

Student products created from information gathered during research should incorporate the higher-level thinking skills of Bloom's Taxonomy:

- **Analyze**
- **Evaluate**
- **Create**

These skills are the best way to ensure that students learn content and information literacy skills, as well as challenge them to think in new ways. Marzano's nine categories of instructional strategies that are most affective in teaching are another resource when constructing final products. (See Figure 1.1 for a complete list of Marzano's nine categories of instructional strategies and Figure 1.2 for Bloom's Taxonomy for Learning, Teaching, and Assessing.)

The following activities integrate the instructional strategies information by Marzano and Bloom, and are activities that require students to analyze, synthesize, and evaluate information.

- **Comparing and contrasting items**
- **Categorizing items**
- **Creating or inventing a new item based on known information**
- **Predicting an event based on known information**
- **Summarizing information learned, in verbal or written form**
- **Teaching others information learned**
- **Revising and editing notes, and adding additional information**
- **Drawing pictures to illustrate information learned**
- **Analyzing and graphing information into a new format, such as a pictograph or bar graph**
- **Creating and completing new graphic organizers with information learned**
- **Acting out information**
- **Creating models of information**
- **Creating analogies or metaphors to information learned**

STEP 6 - RESEARCH MATERIALS

Gather the student materials needed for the research project.

Gathering the needed research materials beforehand will reduce confusion. Caddies or boxes with pencils, erasers, and crayons on each table for the students to use are helpful organizational tools.

Brightly colored sticky notes or highlighted tape are an invaluable trick when conducting research with young learners. Use the sticky notes or tape to highlight specific parts of the text so the student can easily relocate information while transcribing it into his note-taking organizer. (This process saves time by keeping the word highlighted as the student looks back and forth from the text to his notes.) It also provides a concrete illustration that the information he is recording in his notes comes from the text and provides the answer to an information need. Additionally, it saves the sources from pencil marks as the student tracks note-taking progress.

STEP 7 – STUDENT INSTRUCTION

Teach students any necessary information literacy skills prior to research time, such as a problem-solving process or use of a bibliography. Work with students during research time and as they complete their product.

It is imperative that the librarian and teacher work together during research time. Formative assessment should be ongoing during library research. The students should be frequently asked to prove their answers and explain the information they are recording in their notes.

CAUTION: Eager young researchers tend to be very noisy during their time of discovery and research. On the surface, this may be disconcerting to some teachers and librarians. Focus on the content of the students' verbal interactions instead of on the noise level. If the students are discussing their research, aiding each other in locating information, or sharing information that they have discovered, the noise is a reflection of collaborative learning taking place.

We have found that young researchers can work on taking notes from 30 minutes up to an hour. Each research class or group needs to be monitored for time on task. Student behavior will often signal when they are ready to move on. Many times, library research is best divided into two or three sessions in the library.

STEP 8 – STUDENT ASSESSMENT

Complete assessment rubrics to determine student success and to ensure instructional goals have been met.

Assessing student academic success is an important aspect of library research.

In Marzano's *What Works in Schools: Translating Research into Action*, two of the nine highly affective instructional strategies involve monitoring and assessing student progress. Effective instruction involves recognizing and reinforcing progress toward learning goals and student effort. Incorporating formative (on-going) and summative (at completion) assessment into library research with emergent readers is crucial to making a library research project a valuable instructional experience.

Monitor students throughout the project to ensure proper research skills application. Asking students to prove their information, as mentioned in the research skills section of this chapter, is one method of formative assessment. A rubric at the completion of the research project serves as a summative assessment. These rubrics for the teacher and librarian, as well as the students, will help monitor student success. Rubrics should address the instructional goals of the project. (Sample library research rubrics are included in Appendix A of this manual.)

STEP 9 - PROJECT EVALUATION

Evaluate and modify the research project for future use.

At the end of a library research project, the librarian and teacher need to evaluate the project to ensure it was a quality learning experience for the students. This evaluation is most helpful if completed immediately after the project. It is important that the librarian ask for and include teacher feedback in the evaluation process.

Consider whether the project was too easy or too difficult for the students. Ask yourselves whether the instructional goals (curriculum standards, information literacy skills, and technology skills) were adequately met. If they were not met, why not?

Reflect on the aspects of the library research project that worked well. Why did they work well? Conversely, what did not work well? How can changes be made to these aspects to improve the next library research project?

Ask the teacher whether she would consider another library research project for emergent readers. What did she think was valuable in the library research process? What does she think needs to be changed?

IMPLEMENTATION

Now that you are familiar with a step-by-step process for conducting research with emergent readers, it is time to consider if you are ready for this fun and exciting instructional challenge. With strong communication between you and your collaboration partner, perseverance to continue modifying your research projects as you move forward, and eager young researchers, you are well on your way to helping your emergent readers become the most proficient researchers in your school.

Chapters 3-9 contain research projects for you to use as is, or to modify for your specific needs. Each chapter begins with a research project overview followed by supporting documents for student note-taking and product creation. A brief explanation of the layout for chapters 3-9 follows:

RESEARCH PROJECT OVERVIEW

- *Time*—Approximate time needed to complete the library research portion of the project.
- *Instructional Goals*—The general instructional objectives for the particular project highlighted.
- *Integrated Content Standards*—The content curriculum connections for the research project. Refer to Table 1.2, Matrix of Content Standards Integration, for specific content connections.
- *Resources*—A list of possible student resources will provide you with a starting point during your project planning and teacher collaboration. It may also aid in collection development as you work to incorporate library research with emergent readers in your yearly curriculum calendar.
- *Other Student Product Ideas*—At the end of each project overview, we have included other student product ideas.

STUDENT RESEARCH NOTES BOOKLETS AND GRAPHIC ORGANIZERS

After the research project overview, there are at least three different versions of research notes booklets or graphic organizers for your students to use when recording their research information. Each version modifies or extends the skills students need to complete their research notes. Choose the version that best fits your student needs and available resources. Research notes booklets are designed to be copied back-to-back, folded into a booklet, and stapled. Feel free to further modify these booklets and organizers to meet your specific instructional needs.

STUDENT RESEARCH PRODUCT

Included at the end of each chapter is a step-by-step guide for the student research product highlighted under Instructional Goals. We have also included necessary handouts or graphic organizers students will need in order to complete their product, where applicable.

chapter 3

Animal Research Project

RESEARCH PROJECT OVERVIEW

Research Project Title: Animals

Time: 2 hours total, divided into instructionally appropriate blocks of time

Instructional Goals

- Students will conduct research using nonfiction resources to record notes about an animal.
- Students will use a problem-solving process, such as the Big6™ or the Super3™, to guide them through the research project.
- Students will compare and contrast different animals according to physical features, habitats, diet, and other aspects using the *Animal Venn Diagram.*

INTEGRATED CONTENT STANDARDS

(See Table 1.2 Matrix of Content Standards Integration)

- *Benchmarks for Language Arts*
- *Standards for the English Language Arts*
- *Information Literacy Standards for Student Learning*
- *National Science Education Standards: K-4*
- *National Educational Technology Standards for Students*

RESOURCES

PRINT

Various animal sets - Capstone Press' Pebble
Various animal sets - Capstone Press' Pebble Plus
In the Wild series - Raintree's Sprouts
Animals series - Lerner's Pull Ahead Books

ELECTRONIC

Chicago Public Schools: Visiting the Zoo <zone.cps.k12.il.us/Projects/Grade_1/Animals/Activity_14/
        activity_14.html>
Enchanted Learning Animal Printouts <www.enchantedlearning.com>
World Book Online Kids <http://worldbookonline.com/>

OTHER STUDENT PRODUCT IDEAS

- Graph animal facts as a class: How many legs does your animal have? Where does your animal eat?

- Categorize animals by physical features, diet, or habitat.

- Create a new animal. Decide its habitat, physical features, and diet. Have students explain how these things are related to each other.

- Create an animal riddle book in Kid Pix® or MS Word. Students type a "Who Am I?" clue and illustrate with a picture of their animal.

STUDENT RESEARCH NOTES BOOKLETS AND GRAPHIC ORGANIZERS

Figure 3.1 Animal Research version 1

Animal Research
Notes About

Research by

Research completed in the school library

My Bibliography

I found my research information in a book called

The book was written by

Figure 3.2 Animal Research version 1

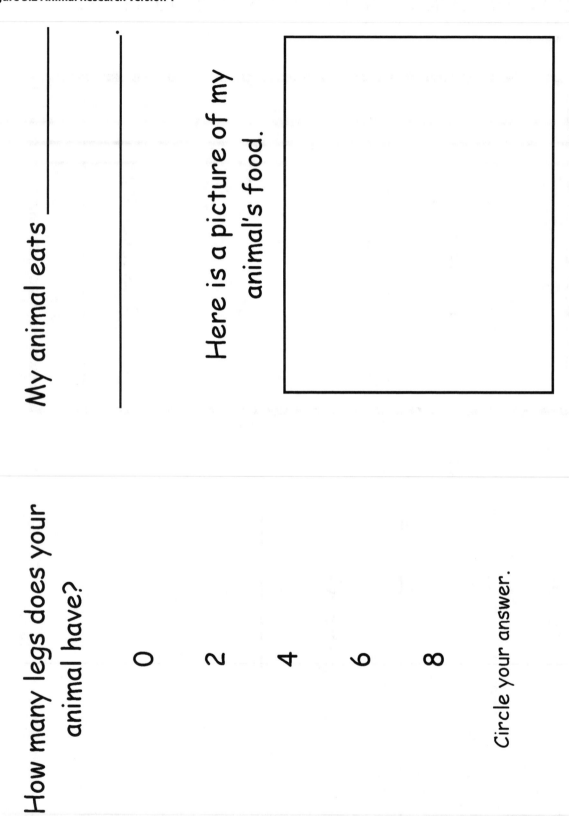

My animal eats _____.

Here is a picture of my animal's food.

How many legs does your animal have?

0

2

4

6

8

Circle your answer.

Figure 3.3 Animal Research version 1

Draw an interesting fact about your animal.

Here is a detailed picture of my animal.

Figure 3.4 Animal Research version 1

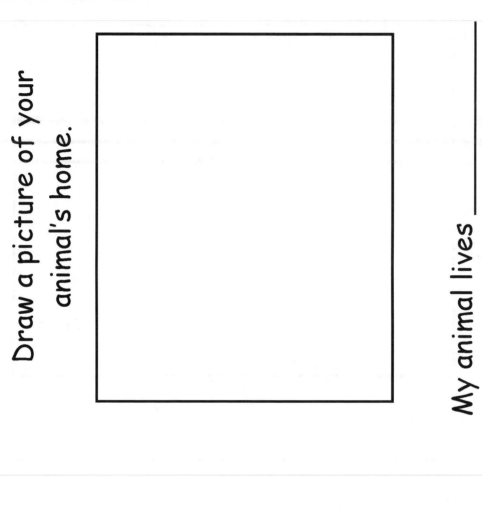

Draw a picture of your animal's home.

My animal lives _____

My animal has

hair or fur

scales

feathers

fins

Circle your answer.

Figure 3.5 Animal Research version 2

Animal Research
Notes About

Research by

Research completed in the school library

My Bibliography

I found my research information in a
book called

The book was written by

Figure 3.6 Animal Research version 2

Here is an interesting fact about my animal.

Here is a detailed picture of my animal.

Figure 3.7 Animal Research version 2

How many legs does your animal have?

0

2

4

6

8

Circle your answer.

Here is more information about my animal's habitat.

My animal is found in the **rain forest.**
Yes ◯   No ◯

My animal is found in the **ocean.**
Yes ◯   No ◯

My animal is found in the **woodlands.**
Yes ◯   No ◯

My animal is found in the **grasslands.**
Yes ◯   No ◯

My animal is found in the **desert.**
Yes ◯   No ◯

Color your answers.

Figure 3.8 Animal Research version 2

Where does your animal live?

in the water

on the ground

in a tree

Draw a picture of your animal's habitat.

5

Here is more information about my animal.

My animal has hair or fur.   Yes◯ No◯

My animal has scales.   Yes◯ No◯

My animal has feathers.   Yes◯ No◯

My animal has fins or flippers.   Yes◯ No◯

Color your answers.

Figure 3.9 Animal Research version 3

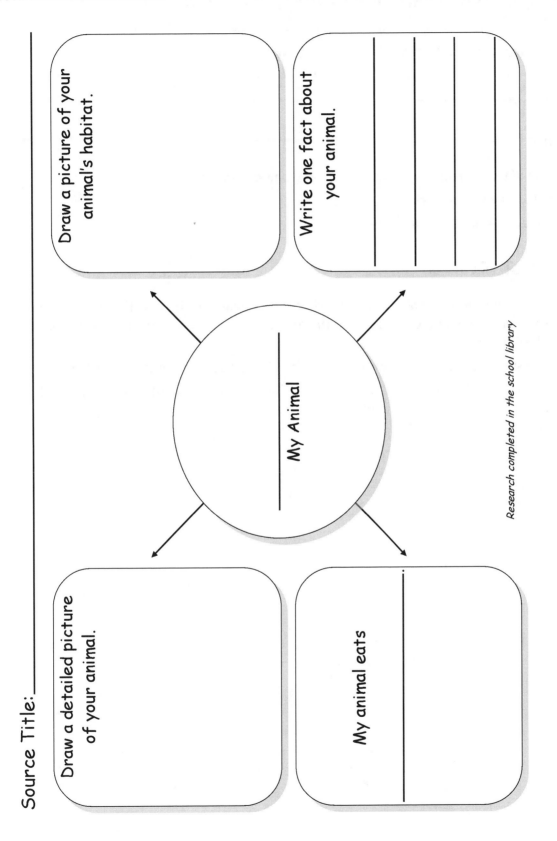

Source Title: _____

Draw a picture of your animal's habitat.

Write one fact about your animal.

My Animal _____

Draw a detailed picture of your animal.

My animal eats _____

Research completed in the school library

STUDENT RESEARCH PRODUCT – ANIMAL VENN DIAGRAM

> **Research Product: Animal Venn Diagram**
>
> **Time:** 20 minutes

MATERIALS

- copies of the *Animal Venn Diagram* for each pair of students
- pencils, crayons, or markers
- completed Animal Research Notes

PRODUCT PROCEDURE

1. Divide students into pairs. Consider whether you want students with similar animals (e.g., both mammals) or students with very different animals (e.g., a snake and a dolphin) together.
2. Have students share their completed Animal Research Notes with each other.
3. Ask each pair to complete the *Animal Venn Diagram* for their animals using their research notes. They may draw or write their information.

Figure 3.10 Animal Research Venn Diagram

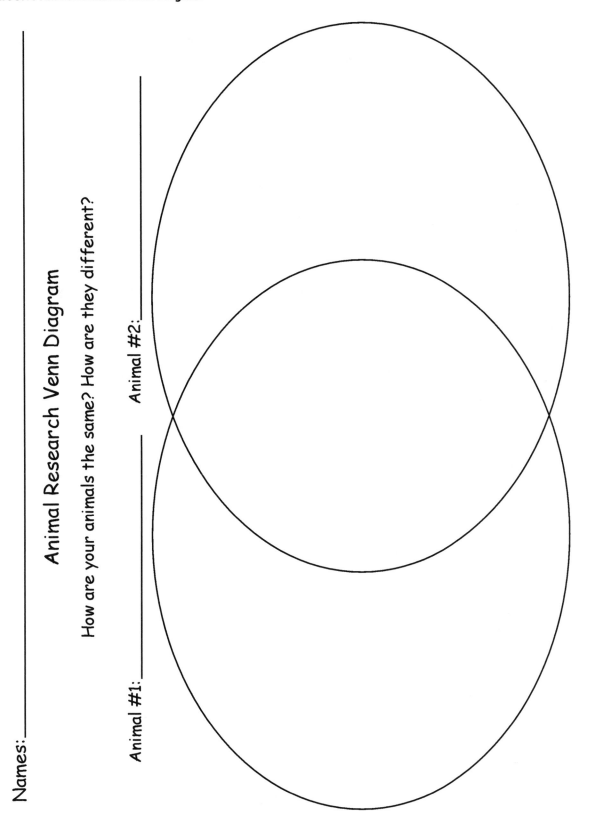

Names: _____

Animal Research Venn Diagram

How are your animals the same? How are they different?

Animal #2: _____

Animal #1: _____

chapter 4

Earth Features Research Project

RESEARCH PROJECT OVERVIEW

Research Project Title: Earth Features

Time: 90 minutes total, divided into instructionally appropriate blocks of time

Instructional Goals

- Students will conduct research using nonfiction resources to record notes about Earth features.
- Students will use a problem-solving process to guide them through the research process.
- Students will create an *Earth Features Riddle Book* with clues describing their Earth feature.

INTEGRATED CONTENT STANDARDS
(See Table 1.2 Matrix of Content Standards Integration)

- *Benchmarks for Language Arts*
- *Standards for the English Language Arts*
- *Information Literacy Standards for Student Learning*
- *National Science Education Standards: K-4*
- *Curriculum Standards for Social Studies*
- *National Educational Technology Standards for Students*

RESOURCES

PRINT
Earth Features series - Capstone Press' Pebble
Landforms series - Heinemann's Acorn
What Do You See series - ABDO's SandCastle

ELECTRONIC
World Book Kids <http://worldbookonline.com>

OTHER STUDENT PRODUCT IDEAS

- Synthesize information into a new graphic organizer using Kid Pix®, Kidspiration®, or paper.
- Create a mural of an Earth feature on large paper and present information to the class.
- Use teacher-selected images and import them into a computer slide show, data bank, or poster.
- Draw Earth feature in Kid Pix® and write a sentence about that Earth feature.

STUDENT RESEARCH NOTES BOOKLETS AND GRAPHIC ORGANIZERS

Figure 4.1 Earth Features Research version 1

Earth Features

Research Notes
About

_____

By

_____

Research completed in the school library

Write an interesting fact about your earth feature.

_____

_____

_____

Bibliography

I found my information in a book.

Book Title: _____

Author: _____

Figure 4.2 Earth Features Research version 1

What could you do if you visited this earth feature?

_____

_____

_____

Here are some words that describe this earth feature.

_____

_____

_____

This is a picture of my earth feature.

It is a _____.

A famous example of this earth feature is called _____.

Table 4.3 Earth Features Research version 2

Name: _____

Earth Features Research Notes

Earth Feature	Picture	Fact

Table 4.4 Library Research with Emergent Readers - Earth Features Research version 2

Bibliography

Circle the book titles you used during your research:

What Are Caves?	*What Are Deserts?*	*What Are Forests?*	*What Are Lakes?*
What Are Mountains?	*What Are Oceans?*	*What Are Rivers?*	*What Are Volcanoes?*

Figure 4.5 Earth Features Research version 3

Name:_____

Earth Features Research Notes

My Earth feature is a _____ .

Draw your Earth feature.

Write one fact about your Earth feature.

_____

_____

_____

Bibliography (Write the title and author of your source.)

_____

STUDENT RESEARCH PRODUCT - EARTH FEATURES RIDDLE BOOK

Research Product: Earth Features Riddle Book

Time: 30-45 minutes

MATERIALS

- copies of *Earth Features Riddle Book* for each student (copy back-to-back and fold in half)
- pencils and crayons
- completed Earth Features Research Notes

PRODUCT PROCEDURE

1. Ask students to review their completed Earth Features Research Notes.
2. Explain that they are going to pretend to visit their Earth feature. They are going to have people guess which Earth feature they are visiting.
3. Brainstorm clues the students may write to hint at the Earth feature they are visiting.
4. Have students complete their *Earth Features Riddle Books*.
5. Display the *Earth Features Riddle Books* so students may work to solve the different riddles.

Where Am I?

This place has _____

_____ •

It looks like _____

_____ •

Bibliography

My research was completed in the school

library using a book called _____

_____ .

Figure 4.6 Earth Features Riddle Book

Figure 4.7 Earth Features Riddle Book

I am visiting

_____.

Here is a picture of me at _____.

chapter 5

Seasons Research Project

RESEARCH PROJECT OVERVIEW

Research Project Title: Seasons

Time: 60 minutes total, divided into instructionally appropriate blocks of time

Instructional Goals

- Students will conduct research using nonfiction resources to record notes about the seasons.
- Students will use a problem-solving process to guide them through the research process.
- Students will compare the seasons by creating a *Seasons Four-Corner Poster.*

INTEGRATED CONTENT STANDARDS
(See Table 1.2 Matrix of Content Standards Integration)

- *Benchmarks for Language Arts*
- *Standards for the English Language Arts*
- *Information Literacy Standards for Student Learning*
- *National Science Education Standards: K-4*
- *Curriculum Standards for Social Studies*
- *National Educational Technology Standards for Students*

RESOURCES
PRINT
Investigate the Seasons series - Capstone Press' Pebble Plus
Seasons series - Capstone Press' Pebble
Seasons series - Heinemann's Read and Learn
Seasons series - Lerner's First Step Nonfiction

ELECTRONIC

Discovery Education *streaming* <http://streaming.discoveryeducation.com>
Zoe's Silly Seasons by Sesame Street <www.sesameworkshop.org/sesamestreet/games/flash.
     php?contentId=111660&>

OTHER STUDENT PRODUCT IDEAS

- After each student researches each of the four seasons, create mobiles with illustrations and facts representing the seasons.

- Create multiple T-charts comparing seasons by animal activities, weather, or human activities; ask students to draw conclusions about how the weather during each season affects animals and humans.

- Create silly season posters where each student creates a season scene with five correct pictorial facts for the season and three incorrect pictorial facts for the season (see Zoe's *Silly Seasons* under Electronic Resources for ideas); have students find the incorrect facts in other posters.

STUDENT RESEARCH NOTES BOOKLETS AND GRAPHIC ORGANIZERS

Figure 5.1 Seasons Research version 1

Season Research Notes About

_____

Research by:

_____

Research completed in the school library

My Bibliography

I found my information in a book called

_____

The book was written by

_____

Figure 5.2 Seasons Research version 1

Circle the picture for your season.

My season is _____.

What is the temperature like during your season? Circle the correct thermometer.

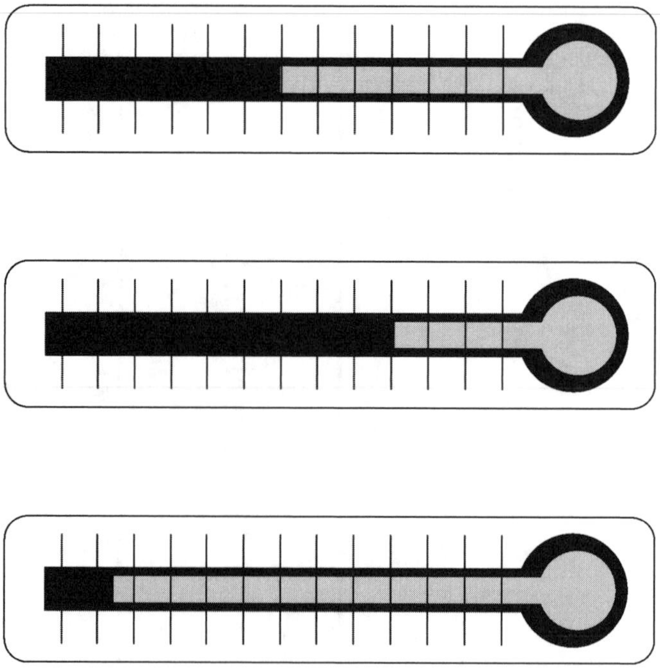

Figure 5.3 Seasons Research version 1

Draw a picture of the things people do during your season.

Draw a picture of the things animals do during your season.

Figure 5.4 Seasons Research version 1

What do the trees look
like during your season?

During my season...

Leaves fall off the   Yes ◯   No ◯
trees during my
season.

Flowers grow   Yes ◯   No ◯
during my season.

Sometimes it snows   Yes ◯   No ◯
during my season.

Many people go to   Yes ◯   No ◯
the beach during my
season.

Table 5.5 Seasons Research version 2

Seasons Research Notes by _____

	Seasons			
	Autumn	Winter	Spring	Summer
What is the weather like?				
What clothing do people wear?				
What do the animals do?				
What is something new you learned?				
Bibliography: What is the title of your source?				

Table 5.6 Seasons Research version 2

How are the seasons alike?

How are the seasons different?

Figure 5.7 Seasons Research version 3

Name:_____

Season Research Notes

My season is_____ .

Draw a picture for your season.

Write one fact about your season.

_____

_____

_____

Bibliography (Write the title and author of your source.)

_____

_____

Research completed in the school library

STUDENT RESEARCH PRODUCT - SEASONS FOUR-CORNER POSTER

> **Research Product: Seasons Four-Corner Poster**
> **Time:** 40 minutes

MATERIALS

- butcher paper or large paper with *Seasons Four-Corner Poster* template
- pencils, crayons, or markers
- completed Seasons Research Notes

PRODUCT PROCEDURE

1. Divide students into pairs or groups of four.
2. Have students share or draw a picture representing their season in the appropriate corner of the *Seasons Four-Corner Poster*.
3. Have students draw or write about the similarities between their seasons in the appropriate boxes.

Figure 5.8 Seasons Four-Corner Poster

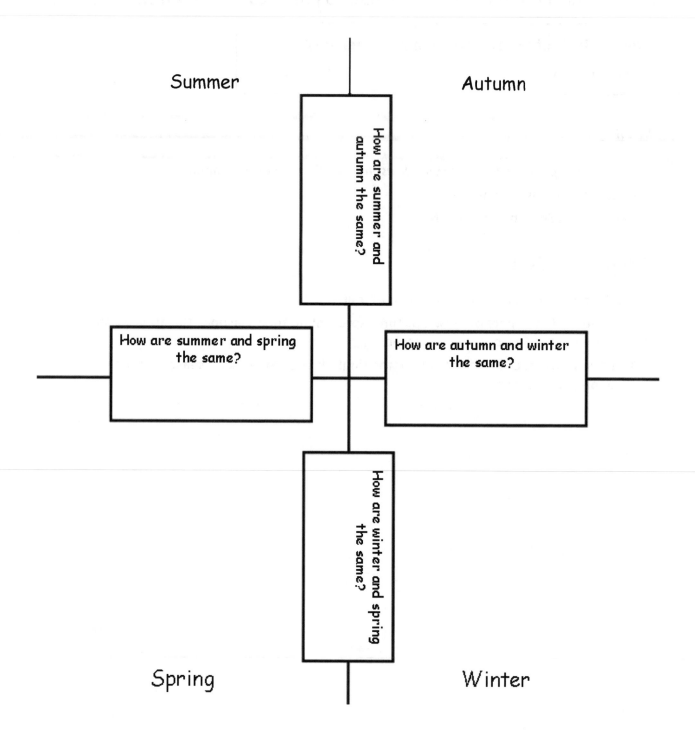

Summer   Autumn

How are summer and autumn the same?

How are summer and spring the same?

How are autumn and winter the same?

How are winter and spring the same?

Spring   Winter

chapter 6

Plants
Research Project

RESEARCH PROJECT OVERVIEW

Research Project Title: Plants

Time: 90 minutes total, divided into instructionally appropriate blocks of time

Instructional Goals

- Students will conduct research using nonfiction resources and observations to record notes about plants.
- Students will use a problem-solving process to guide them through the research process.
- Students will create a *Plant Counting Book*, which describes the parts of a plant.

INTEGRATED CONTENT STANDARDS *(See Table 1.2 Matrix of Content Standards Integration)*

- *Benchmarks for Language Arts*
- *Standards for the English Language Arts*
- *Information Literacy Standards for Student Learning*
- *National Science Education Standards: K-4*
- *National Educational Technology Standards for Students*

OTHER STUDENT PRODUCT IDEAS

- Create a class slideshow where each student contributes a slide about one plant part
- Draw and label the parts of a plant using Kid Pix®
- Dissect real plants and label their flowers, roots, stems, fruit, and seeds
- Under student guidance, take digital pictures of plants and plant parts around the school, print the pictures, and have students label the plant parts

RESOURCES
PRINT
Growing Flowers series - Capstone Press' Pebble
Plant Parts series - Capstone Press' Pebble Plus
Plants series - Heinemann's Read and Learn

ELECTRONIC
Discovery Education *streaming* <http://streaming.discoveryeducation.com>
World Book Kids <http://worldbookonline.com>

STUDENT RESEARCH NOTES BOOKLETS AND GRAPHIC ORGANIZERS

Figure 6.1 Plants Research version 1

Research Notes About _____

by _____

Research completed in the school library

Bibliography

Author: _____

Title: _____

Research Notes About _____

by _____

Research completed in the school library

Bibliography

Author: _____

Title: _____

Figure 6.2 Plants Research version 1

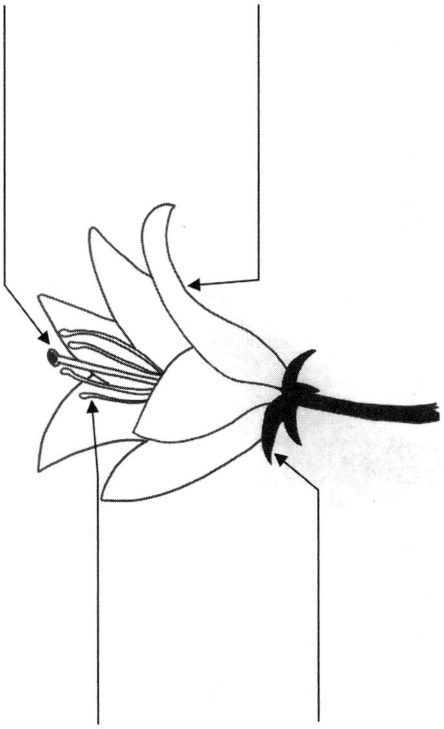

Draw a picture of the plant on the table. Label its parts.

| flower |
| leaf |
| root |
| stem |

Label the flower.

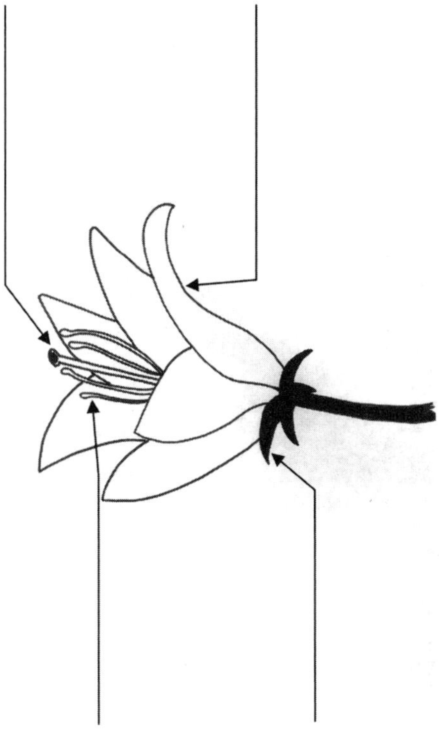

Draw a picture of the plant on the table. Label its parts.

| flower |
| leaf |
| root |
| stem |

Label the flower.

Figure 6.3 Plants Research version 1

What does pollen look like?

_____
_____
_____
_____
_____

What does pollen look like?

_____
_____
_____
_____
_____

List 3 things plants need to live.

1.

2.

3.

List 3 things plants need to live.

1.

2.

3.

What does a stem do?

_____
_____
_____
_____
_____

4

Look at the pictures of leaves.
Draw and color 3 different
types of leaves.

Leaf 1

What does a stem do?

_____
_____
_____
_____
_____

4

Look at the pictures of leaves.
Draw and color 3 different
types of leaves.

Leaf 1

Figure 6.5 Plants Research version 1

Leaf 2	Leaf 3	Leaf 2	Leaf 3

What does a root do?

_____

_____

_____

_____

What does a root do?

_____

_____

_____

_____

Figure 6.6 Plants Research version 1

What does a seed do?

Draw and color 3 types of seeds.

Research with Emergent Readers– Plant Research version 1 (Figure 6.6) 6

What does a seed do?

Draw and color 3 types of seeds.

Figure 6.7 Plants Research version 2

Research Notes
About

_____

By

_____

Research completed in the school library

Draw or write an interesting fact about plants.

Bibliography

I found my information in a series of plant books written by the author:

_____

Figure 6.8 Plants Research version 2

Draw and color 3 different types of leaves.

Draw 1 kind of root that people eat.

3

Draw a picture of a plant. Label the parts of the plant.

flower
leaves
roots
stem
seeds

Draw and color 2 different kinds of flowers.

Figure 6.9 Plants Research version 3

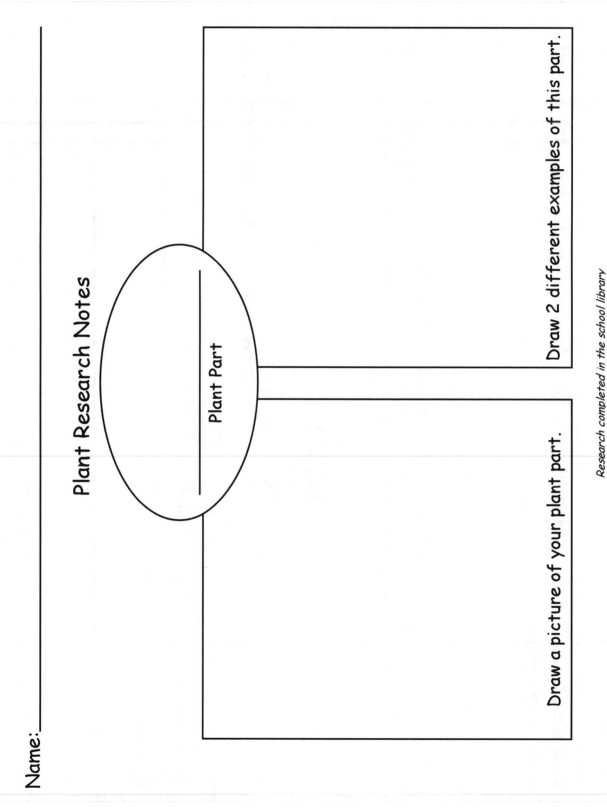

Plant Research Notes

Name: _____

Plant Part

Draw a picture of your plant part.

Draw 2 different examples of this part.

Research completed in the school library

Figure 6.10 Plants Research version 3

Why is this part important to a plant?

Write or draw an interesting fact about this plant part.

Bibliography- What source did you use?

I got my research information from:

Title: _____

Author: _____

STUDENT RESEARCH PRODUCT - PLANT COUNTING BOOK

Research Product: Plant Counting Book

Time: 45-60 minutes

MATERIALS

- *Plant Counting Book* copies for each student
- completed Plants Research Notes
- pencils, crayons, or markers

PRODUCT PROCEDURE

1. Cut the *Plant Counting Book* copies in half and staple the pages together into a book.
2. Have each student draw the appropriate parts of a plant on each page of their *Plant Counting Book*.
3. As an added challenge, have students write one fact about each part of the plant or plants in general on the pages in the *Plant Counting Book*.
4. Have students transfer their bibliography information from their Plants Research Notes to their final product, their *Plant Counting Book*.

Figure 6.11 Plants Counting Book

My Plant
Counting Book

by

_____

- -

1 seed

2

Figure 6.12 Plants Counting Book

1 seed and 2 roots

3

1 seed, 2 roots, and 3 stems

Library Research with Emergent Readers- Plants Counting Book (Figure 6.12)

4

Figure 6.13 Plants Counting Book

1 seed, 2 roots, 3 stems, and 4 leaves

5

1 seed, 2 roots, 3 stems, 4 leaves, and
5 flowers

Library Research with Emergent Readers- Plants Counting Book (Figure 6.13) 6

Figure 6.14 Plants Counting Book

1 seed, 2 roots, 3 stems, 4 leaves, and 5 flowers make 1 plant. Label the parts of your plant.

7

- -

Bibliography

_____

_____

From *Library Research with Emergent Readers: Meeting Standards through Collaboration* by Christa Harker and Dorette Putonti. Columbus, OH: Linworth Publishing, Inc. Copyright © 2008.

chapter 7

Community Helpers Research Project

RESEARCH PROJECT OVERVIEW

> **Research Project Title: Community Helpers**
>
> **Time:** 80 minutes total, divided into instructionally appropriate blocks of time
>
> **Instructional Goals**
>
> - Students will conduct research using nonfiction resources to record notes about community helpers.
>
> - Students will use a problem-solving process to guide them through the research process.
>
> - Students will write a postcard to their community helper thanking them for their hard work.

INTEGRATED CONTENT STANDARDS
(See Table 1.2 Matrix of Content Standards Integration)

- *Benchmarks for Language Arts*
- *Standards for the English Language Arts*
- *Information Literacy Standards for Student Learning*
- *Curriculum Standards for Social Studies*
- *National Educational Technology Standards for Students*

RESOURCES

PRINT
Community Helpers series - Capstone Press' Bridgestone Books
Community Helpers series - Welcome Books
Helpers in Our Community series - Capstone Press' Pebble
This Is What I Want to Be series - Heinemann's Read and Learn

ELECTRONIC
Community Club by Scholastic <www.teacher.scholastic.com/commclub/index.htm>

OTHER STUDENT PRODUCT IDEAS

- Dress in the uniform of a community helper and present information to the class
- Create a "Help Wanted" poster for a community helper's job
- Interview community helpers in the school, such as the nurse, safety officer, and custodian; report information learned to the class

STUDENT RESEARCH NOTES BOOKLETS AND GRAPHIC ORGANIZERS

Figure 7.1 Community Helpers Research version 1

A Community Helper Notes

About

Here is a picture of my community helper working.

Research by

Research completed in the school library

My Bibliography

I found my research information in a book called

That book was written by

Figure 7.2 Community Helpers Research version 1

Here are some interesting facts about my community helper.

What does your community helper do?

Figure 7.3 Community Helpers Research version 1

Who does your community
helper help?

adults   Yes ◯   No ◯

children   Yes ◯   No ◯

animals   Yes ◯   No ◯

Here is a picture of my
community helper's uniform.

Figure 7.4 Community Helpers Research version 1

Here are some of the tools my community helper uses.

Where does your community helper work?

My community helper works in

Draw a picture of where your community helper works.

From *Library Research with Emergent Readers: Meeting Standards through Collaboration* by Christa Harker and Dorette Putonti. Columbus, OH: Linworth Publishing, Inc. Copyright © 2008.

Figure 7.5 Community Helpers Research version 2

Here is a picture of where my community helper works.

My Bibliography

I found my research information in a book called ____________________

____

A Community Helper Notes About

____

Here is a picture of my community helper working.

Research by

____

Research completed in the school library

Figure 7.6 Community Helpers Research version 2

Who does your community helper help?

adults   Yes ◯   No ◯

children   Yes ◯   No ◯

animals   Yes ◯   No ◯

Here are some of the tools my community helper uses.

Figure 7.7 Community Helpers Research version 3

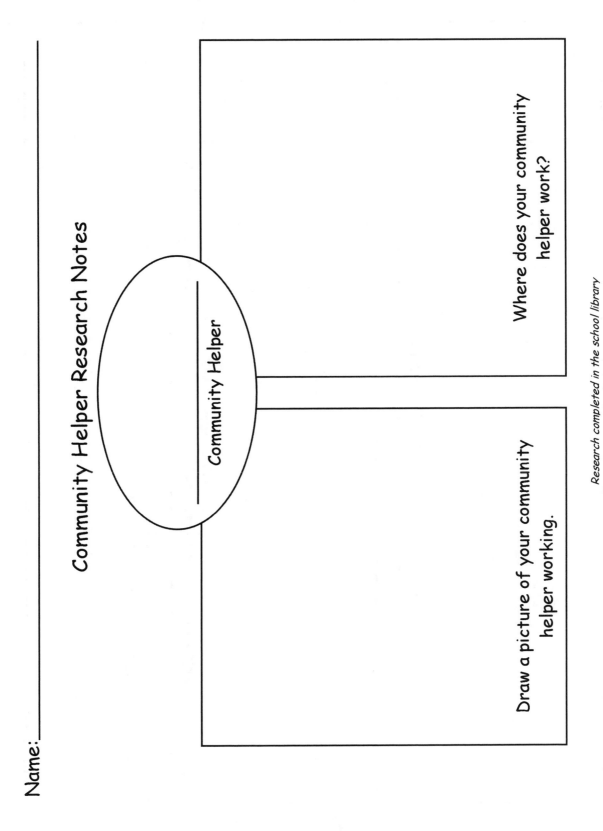

Name: _____

Community Helper Research Notes

Community Helper

Where does your community helper work?

Draw a picture of your community helper working.

Research completed in the school library

Figure 7.8 Community Helpers Research version 3

How does this community helper help our community?

Write or draw an interesting fact about your community helper.

I got my research information from:

Title: _____

Author: _____

Bibliography- What source did you use?

Figure 7.9 Community Helpers Research version 4

Name:_____

Community Helper Research Notes

My community helper is a_____

_____ .

Draw your community helper working. Include the tools your community helper uses.

Write one fact about your community helper.

_____

_____

Bibliography (Write the title and author of your source.)

_____

_____

Research completed in the school library

STUDENT RESEARCH PRODUCT – COMMUNITY HELPER POSTCARD

> **Research Product: Community Helper Postcard**
>
> **Time:** 30-45 minutes

MATERIALS

- one copy of *Community Helper Postcard* for each student, copied on white card stock
- pencils, crayons, or markers
- completed Community Helper Research Notes

PRODUCT PROCEDURE

1. As a class, brainstorm the ways different community helpers help a community. Students should use their completed Community Helper Research Notes to help them with ideas. Make a list of key ideas and words for the students to reference.

2. Ask each student to write or dictate a postcard to the community helper they researched. Blank postcards may be used for students to draw instead of write their information.

3. On the front of the postcard, students should draw and color a picture showing information about the community helper that they learned during their research.

4. If possible, deliver the community helper postcards to appropriate community helpers in the community.

Figure 7.10 Community Helpers Postcard

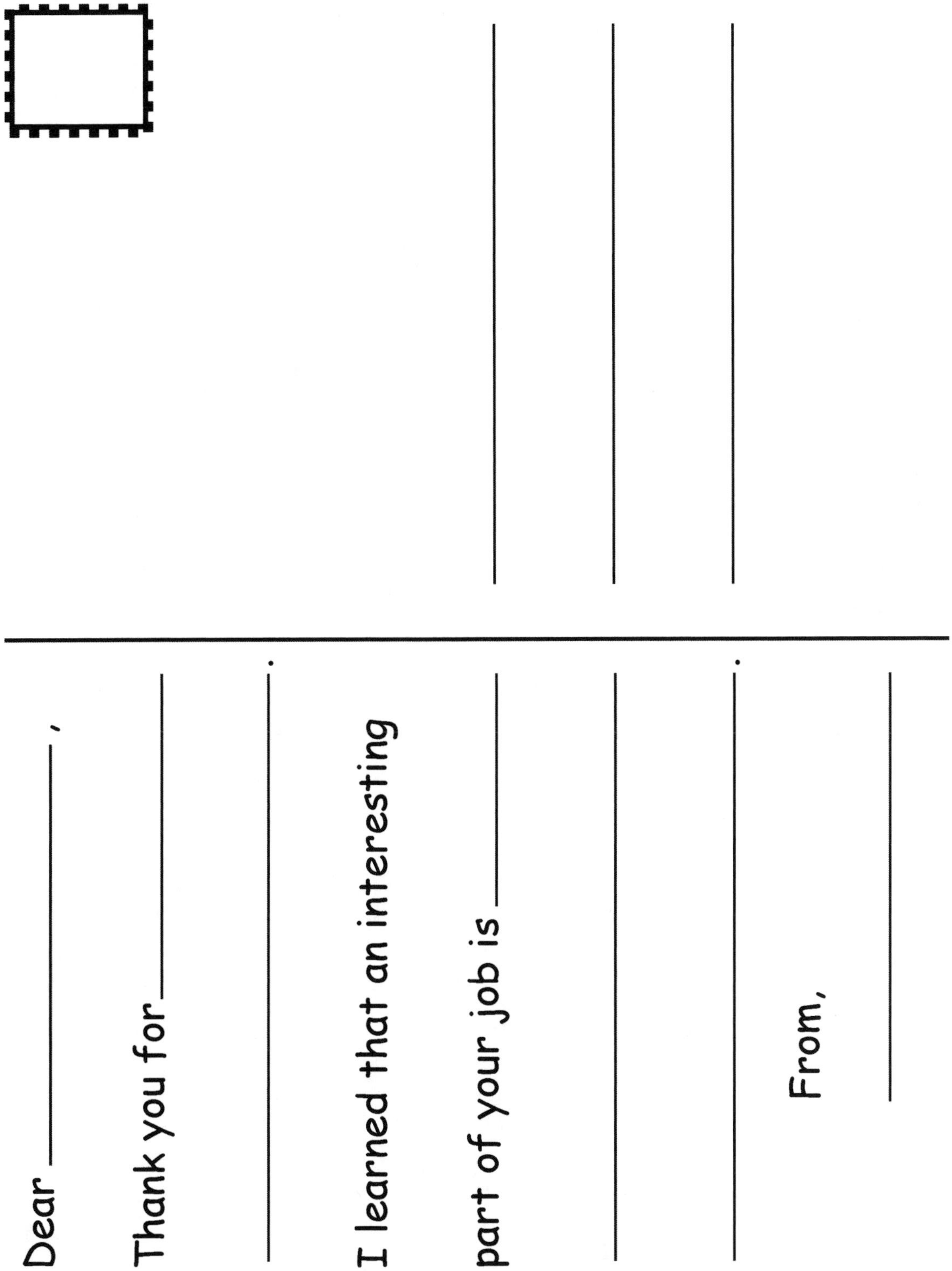

Dear _____,

Thank you for _____.

I learned that an interesting part of your job is _____.

From,
_____

chapter 8:

American Symbols Research Project

RESEARCH PROJECT OVERVIEW

Research Project Title: American Symbols

Time: 45 minutes total, divided into instructionally appropriate blocks of time

Instructional Goals

- Students will conduct research using nonfiction resources to record notes about American symbols.
- Students will use a problem-solving process to guide them through the research process.
- Students will create a Kid Pix® picture that illustrates the American symbol and provides facts about the symbol.

INTEGRATED CONTENT STANDARDS
(See Table 1.2 Matrix of Content Standards Integration)

- *Benchmarks for Language Arts*
- *Standards for the English Language Arts*
- *Information Literacy Standards for Student Learning*
- *Curriculum Standards for Social Studies*
- *National Educational Technology Standards for Students*

RESOURCES
PRINT
American Symbols series - Lerner's Pull Ahead Books
American Symbols series - Welcome Books
Symbols of Freedom series - Heinemann's First Library

Kidport Reference Library: American Icons <www.kidport.com/RefLib/UsaHistory/AmericanIcons/
   AmericanIconIndex.htm>

World Book Kids <http://worldbookonline.com/>

OTHER STUDENT PRODUCT IDEAS

- Create a Kidspiration® web of facts about the American symbol

- Draw the American symbol on a paper bag; draw or write facts about the symbol on slips of paper and put them in the bag. Use this information to present the American symbol to the class.

- Create an art gallery of framed American symbols drawn by students; have students act as docents to lead visitors through the art gallery

- Create a bookmark about the American symbol to copy and handout in the library

STUDENT RESEARCH NOTES BOOKLETS AND GRAPHIC ORGANIZERS

Figure 8.1 American Symbols Research version 1

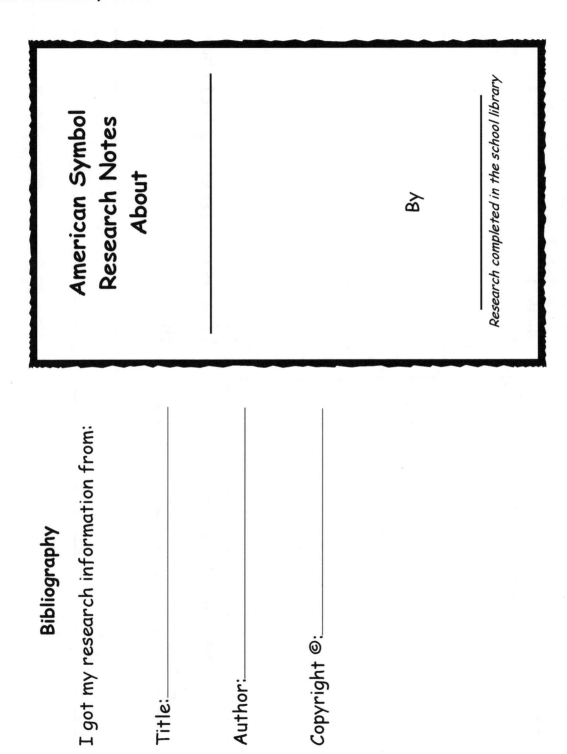

Figure 8.2 American Symbols Research version 1

Draw where people can see this symbol.

What is an interesting fact about this symbol?

_____

_____

_____

Draw a picture of this American symbol.

Why is this symbol important?

_____

_____

_____

Figure 8.3 American Symbols Research version 2

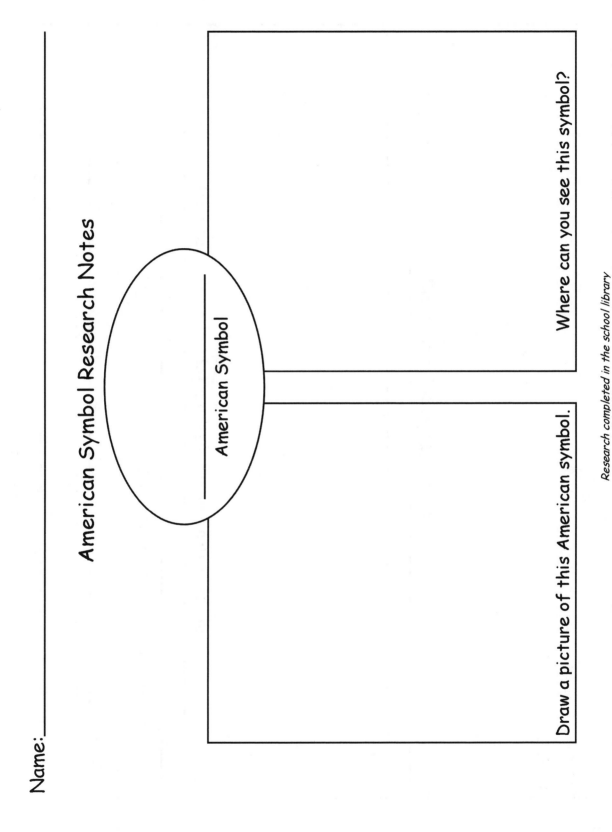

Name: _____

American Symbol Research Notes

American Symbol

Where can you see this symbol?

Draw a picture of this American symbol.

Research completed in the school library

Figure 8.4 American Symbols Research version 2

Why is this symbol important?

Write or draw an interesting fact about this symbol.

I got my research information from:

Title: _____

Author: _____

Bibliography- What source did you use?

Figure 8.5 American Symbols Research version 3

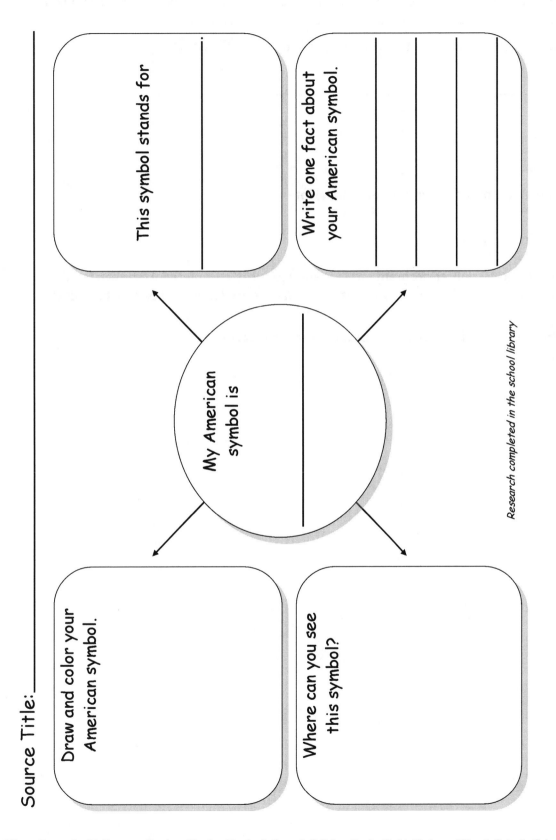

Source Title: _____

This symbol stands for _____

Write one fact about your American symbol.

My American symbol is

Draw and color your American symbol.

Where can you see this symbol?

Research completed in the school library

Research Product: American Symbol Kid Pix® Pictures

Time: 45-60 minutes

MATERIALS

- Kid Pix®
- completed American Symbols Research Notes

PRODUCT PROCEDURE

1. Using the computer program Kid Pix® and students' completed American Symbols Research Notes, have each student draw their symbol and type one fact about that symbol.

2. Print student products and display or create a class book.

chapter 9

Five Senses Research Project

RESEARCH PROJECT OVERVIEW

Research Project Title: Five Senses

Time: 40 minutes total, divided into instructionally appropriate blocks of time

Instructional Goals

- Students will conduct research using nonfiction resources to record notes about one or more of the five senses.
- Students will use a problem-solving process to guide them through the research process.
- Students will complete the *My Senses* graphic organizer synthesizing their notes about each of the five senses.

INTEGRATED CONTENT STANDARDS *(See Table 1.2 Matrix of Content Standards Integration)*

- *Benchmarks for Language Arts*
- *Standards for the English Language Arts*
- *Information Literacy Standards for Student Learning*
- *National Science Education Standards: K-4*
- *National Educational Technology Standards for Students*

OTHER STUDENT PRODUCT IDEAS

- **Create a play where students act out using one or more of the five senses**
- **Create a matching game on index cards where students match a sense to the correct part of the body, have students play as a concentration game**
- **Draw a safety poster that illustrates why a particular sense is important to keeping children safe**

RESOURCES

PRINT

The Senses series - Capstone Press' Pebble
Super Senses series - Heinemann's Read and Learn

ELECTRONIC

Harcourt School Publishers - Sense-Ational <www.harcourtschool.com/activity/senses/index.htm>

Figure 9.1 Five Senses Research version 1

Research Notes About

_____

by _____

Completed in the Library

Bibliography

I used this book for my research notes.

Author: _____

Book Title: _____

Library Research with Emergent Readers– Five Senses version 1 (Figure 9.1)

8

Research Notes About

_____

by _____

Completed in the Library

Bibliography

I used this book for my research notes.

Author: _____

Book Title: _____

note taking form

Draw another fact you learned about this sense.

Draw another fact you learned about this sense.

I am researching the sense of

smelling

tasting

touching

hearing

seeing

(Circle your answer.)

I am researching the sense of

smelling

tasting

touching

hearing

seeing

(Circle your answer.)

Figure 9.3 Five Senses Research version 1

Why is this sense useful?

_____

3

Why is this sense useful?

_____

3

This is a picture of one way I can use this sense.

6

Library Research with Emergent Readers– Five Senses version 1 (Figure 9.3)

This is a picture of one way I can use this sense.

From *Library Research with Emergent Readers: Meeting Standards through Collaboration* by Christa Harker and Dorette Putonti. Columbus, OH: Linworth Publishing, Inc. Copyright © 2008.

Figure 9.4 Five Senses Research version 1

What part of the body do people use with this sense?

○ eyes

○ ears

○ hands

○ tongue

○ nose

(Color in the correct circle.)

Draw a picture of the part of the body people use with this sense.

What part of the body do people use with this sense?

○ eyes

○ ears

○ hands

○ tongue

○ nose

(Color in the correct circle.)

Draw a picture of the part of the body people use with this sense.

Table 9.5 Five Senses Research version 2

Name: _____

Five Senses Research Notes

Sense	Body Part Used	Why is this sense useful?

Table 9.6 Five Senses Research version 2

Bibliography

I used a series of books about the five senses. The author is _____

Figure 9.7 Five Senses Research version 3

Name:_____

Sense Research Notes

My sense is_____ .

Draw the part of our body we use for this sense.

Write one fact about your sense.

_____

_____

_____

Bibliography (Write the title and author of your source.)

_____

_____

Research completed in the school library

STUDENT RESEARCH PRODUCT – FIVE SENSES GRAPHIC ORGANIZER

Research Product: Five Senses Graphic Organizer
Time: 30-45 minutes

MATERIALS

- *My Senses* graphic organizer copy for each student
- completed Five Senses Research Notes
- pencils, crayons, or markers

PRODUCT PROCEDURE

1. Students use their Five Senses Research Notes to draw the body parts people use for their senses on the *My Senses* graphic organizer. They should include eyes, ears, nose, mouth, and skin (e.g., hands) on the graphic organizer.
2. Have students label each body part with the corresponding sense. For example, they should label the eyes with "seeing" or "sight."
3. Students should copy their bibliographic information from their Five Senses Research Notes to their final product.

Figure 9.8 Five Senses Graphic Organizer

Name: _____

My Senses

Use your Senses Research Notes to draw each part of your body that you use with your senses. Label each sense with the correct body part.

Bibliography

appendix A -

Assessment Rubrics

Figure A.1 Student Self-Evaluation Research Rubric version 1

Self-Evaluation Research Rubric

Name: _____

	Always	Some	None
I took notes using my source. I can prove it.	☺	☺	☹
I followed directions.	☺	☺	☹
I finished my research notes.	☺	☺	☹
I finished my project using my research notes.	☺	☺	☹

During my research, I learned...

Self-Evaluation Research Rubric

Name: _____

	Always	Some	None
I used my source to find my information.	:)	:|	:(
I took notes using my source. I can prove it.	:)	:|	:(
I followed directions.	:)	:|	:(
I finished my research notes.	:)	:|	:(
I finished my project using my research notes.	:)	:|	:(

During my research, I learned... _____

_____

Student Assessment Research Rubric

Name: _____

	Always	Some	None
Student found needed information in resource.	○	○	○
Student recorded correct and accurate information in research notes.	○	○	○
Student followed directions, answering questions in appropriate format.	○	○	○
Student completed research notes.	○	○	○
Student used research notes in final product.	○	○	○

Additional Comments: _____

_____

_____

appendix B

Library Research Project Planning And Collaboration Checklist

Planning Worksheet
Research for Emergent Readers

Research Project Title:

Grade Level: Date for Project:

Length of time in classroom:
Length of time in library:
Length of time in computer lab:

Instructional Goals
What do you want the students to learn during this research project?

How will you assess student success?

How will you integrate technology into this research project?

Will students work individually, in pairs, in small groups, or as a class?

Instructional Standards
Which content standards are the main focus for this research project?

Which information literacy standards are the main focus for this project?

Which other content standards will be integrated into this project?

☐Early Literacy   ☐Math
☐Language Arts   ☐Technology
☐Science   ☐Art
☐Social Studies   ☐Music
☐_____   ☐_____

Collaboration Checklist
Complete attached collaboration checklist prior to the research project.

Project Evaluation
Reflect on these questions after the research project is completed.
Were instructional goals met? Why or why not?

What worked well during this project?

What needs to be changed for the next project?

From *Library Research with Emergent Readers: Meeting Standards through Collaboration* by Christa Harker and Dorette Putonti. Columbus, OH: Linworth Publishing, Inc. Copyright © 2008.

Collaboration Checklist
Research for Emergent Readers

Research Project Title:

Grade Level: Date for Project:

Task	Librarian	Teacher
Create student note-taking organizer (booklet, worksheet, graphic organizer)		
Create assessment rubric		
Gather research sources (books, web sites, online resources, encyclopedias, etc.)		
Gather materials (crayons, pencils, sticky notes, etc.)		
Copy student note-taking organizer		
Teach introductory content needed		
Teach research/information literacy skills needed		
Teach technology skills needed		
Monitor student progress		
Assess student success		
Evaluate project for future use		

appendix C

Student Resources For Primary Research Projects

Table C.1 Student Resources for Primary Research Projects *

ABDO Publishing Company
4940 Viking Drive; Edina, Minnesota 55432
1-800-800-1312
<www.abdopub.com>
Series: *SandCastle*

Capstone Press
P.O. Box 669; Mankato, Minnesota 56002-0669
1-800-747-4992
<www.capstonepress.com>
Series: *Bridgestone Books, Pebble Books, Pebble Plus Books*

Children's Press
90 Old Sherman Turnpike; Danbury, Connecticut 06816
1-800-621-1115
<Librarypublishing.scholastic.com>
Series: *Welcome Books*

Heinemann Library
6277 Sea Harbor Dr., 5th Floor; Orlando, Florida 32887
1-888-454-2279
<www.heinemannlibrary.com>
Series: *Acorn, First Library, Read and Learn*

Lerner Publishing Group
1251 Washington Ave. North; Minneapolis, Minnesota 55401-1036
1-800-328-4929
<www.lernerclassroom.com>
Series: *First Step Nonfiction, Pull Ahead Books*

Raintree
6277 Sea Harbor Dr., 5th Floor; Orlando, Florida 32887
1-888-363-4266
<www.raintreelibrary.com>
Series: *Sprouts*

* A version of this table first appeared in Harker, Christa and Dorette Putonti. "Hook Them with Research: Luring Primary Teachers with Early Literacy Skills." Knowledge Quest. 33.2 (2004): 40-44.

Works Cited

American Association of School Librarians. *Standards for the 21st- Century Learner*. Chicago: American Library Association, 2007.

American Association of School Librarians, and Association for Educational Communications and Technology. *Information Literacy Standards for Student Learning*. Chicago: American Library Association, 1998.

Anderson, Lorin W., et al. *Taxonomy for Learning, Teaching and Assessing: A Revision of Bloom's Taxonomy of Educational Objectives*. Boston: Allyn & Bacon, 2000.

Benchmarks for Language Arts. Mid-continent Research for Education and Learning. June 2, 2006 <www.mcrel.org/standards-benchmarks>.

Harker, Christa and Dorette Putonti. "Hook Them with Research: Luring Primary Teachers with Early Literacy Skills." *Knowledge Quest*. 33.2 (2004): 40-44.

Lance, Keith Curry and David Loertscher. *Powering Achievement: School Library Media Programs Make a Difference*. San Jose: Hi Willow Research & Publishing, 2001.

Learning Domains or Bloom's Taxonomy. June 1, 2006 <www.nwlink.com/~donclark/hrd/bloom.html>.

Loetscher, David V. *Taxonomies of the School Library Media Program*. San Jose: Hi Willow Research and Publishing, 2000.

Loertscher, David V., Carol Koechlin, and Sandi Zwaan. *Ban Those Bird Units: 15 Models For Teaching and Learning in Information-rich and Technology-rich Environments*. Salt Lake City: Hi Willow Research and Publishing, 2005.

Marzano, Robert J. *What Works in Schools: Translating Research into Action*. Alexandria: Association for Supervision and Curriculum Development, 2003.

Marzano, Robert J., Debra J. Pickering, and Jane E. Pollock. *Classroom Instruction that Works: Research-based Strategies for Increasing Student Achievement*. Alexandria: Association for Supervision and Curriculum Development, 2001.

Miller, Donna. *The Standards-Based Integrated Library: A Collaborative Approach for Aligning the Library Program with the Classroom Curriculum*. Worthington: Linworth Publishing Inc., 2004.

National Council for the Social Studies. *Curriculum Standards for Social Studies.* Washington, D.C.: National Council for the Social Studies, 1994.

National Science Education Standards: K-4. May 22, 2006. <www.nap.edu/readingroom/books/nses/6c. html>.

National Standards for History (K-4). National Center for History in Schools. June 1, 2006 <nchs.ucla. edu/standards/toc.html>.

Standards for the English Language Arts. National Council of Teachers of English and International Reading Association. June 2, 2006 <www.ncte.org>.

Texas Essential Knowledge and Skills. Texas Education Agency Office of Curriculum and Professional Development. June 5, 2006 <http://www.tea.state.tx.us/teks/index.html>.

Index